DEEP

self-reflection one day at a time

/ /

Is the life that I am living the life I want to be living?

day one

/ /

What is one thing I could start doing today to improve the quality of my life?

/ /

When was the last time I told myself 'I am enough'?

day three

/ /

Am I a source of inspiration for my friends and family?

/ /

What is something that overwhelms me?

/ /

Would I consider myself on the right path?

/ /

What is something I love?

day seven

/ /

Am I proud of the person I am today?

/ /

Who is someone I love?

/ /

Is it difficult for me to trust others?

day ten

/ /

Do I love myself?

day eleven

/ /

What do I fear the most?

/ /

Do I love my job?

/ /

What am I thankful for?

day fourteen

/ /

Do I fear death?

day fifteen

/ /

What do I like the most about myself?

/ /

What is something I love?

day seventeen

/ /

What is something I see myself doing ten years from now?

/ /

What is something I want to let go of, but can't?

day nineteen

/ /

Is there something or someone stopping me from becoming who I want to be?

/ /

Do I feel like I have missed out on anything in life?

/ /

Would I consider myself damaged?

/ /

Do I feel stuck with where I am at in life?

/ /

What is stopping me from becoming successful?

day twenty-four

/ /

Am I holding onto something I need to let go of?

/ /

What have I given up on that I now regret?

/ /

What is something I need to work on to better myself?

/ /

What is something that worries me?

/ /

Who is someone I miss?

day twenty-nine

/ /

Is it more important to me to be loved or to love?

day thirty

/ /

How many true friends do I have?

day thirty-one

/ /

What is something I take for granted?

/ /

What is a moment I will never forget in my life?

/ /

What is something or who is someone I could not imagine life without?

/ /

Who was my first true love?

/ /

Do I have any toxic relationships - why are they still involved in my life?

/ /

Who inspires me to become the person I want to be?

/ /

What is something I want to do, but will never have the courage to do?

/ /

What has been my biggest mistake in life?

/ /

What have I learned from my biggest mistake?

/ /

Do I spend more time at work than I do with the people I love - why?

/ /

If I could change anything about my life, what would it be?

/ /

How would I spend my favorite day?

/ /

Do I consider myself to have a privileged life?

/ /

Am I truly happy?

/ /

Why do I matter to the people that care about me?

/ /

Who do I think loves me the most?

/ /

What is a piece of advice I would give to someone I care about?

/ /

Who is someone I want to talk to that I no longer can - what would I say?

/ /

What is something I will never give up?

/ /

Who is someone I regret having a relationship with?

/ /

What is the most important thing to me?

/ /

If I were to die today, would I be happy with my life?

/ /

When is the last time I went out of my comfort zone?

/ /

Who do I enjoy to be around?

/ /

When I am in pain (mentally or physically), who do I want to comfort me?

/ /

How many friends do I trust with my life?

day fifty-seven

/ /

What is something I wish people knew about me?

day fifty-eight

/ /

What is my biggest secret?

day fifty-nine

/ /

Who has the biggest influence on my life?

/ /

What is something that brings peace into my life?

/ /

Do I fear the health of my parents?

/ /

If there is one thing I could do for the rest of my life, what would it be?

day sixty-three

/ /

Do I consider myself lucky to be where I am today?

/ /

What was my mood when I woke up today - why?

/ /

What is one thing I am going to work on today to better myself?

/ /

Is there something I regret saying that hurt someone?

/ /

Do I fear that I will not meet my soulmate?

/ /

When was the last time I laughed so hard I could barely catch my breath?

/ /

What is my favorite memory from when I was a child?

/ /

What is something I do every single day that I enjoy?

/ /

What makes me smile no matter what?

day seventy-two

/ /

Do I want more in life?

/ /

Have I ever failed someone?

day seventy-four

/ /

What was the last thing I truly worked hard for?

/ /

Who is someone I gave up on that I regret giving up on?

/ /

Do I believe there is someone out there for everyone?

/ /

What is my biggest insecurity?

/ /

What is something I will never forget?

day seventy-nine

/ /

Why do I matter?

/ /

Am I putting enough effort into my relationships?

/ /

Am I taking care of myself mentally and physically?

/ /

Am I where I want to be finanically?

/ /

What is something I never want to go through again?

day eighty-four

/ /

What do I need to let go of, but can't find myself to do so?

/ /

What impact do I want to leave behind?

/ /

If I could turn back time, what would I do differently?

/ /

What is the most spontaneous thing I have ever done?

/ /

What advice would I say to my past self?

/ /

If I had more time to do what I love - what would I do?

day ninety

/ /

What keeps me grounded?

/ /

What is my favorite thing about myself?

/ /

Which relationship matters most to me?

/ /

Am I avoiding any confrontations - why?

/ /

What motivates me to get up for the day?

/ /

Who do I hope to be like?

day ninety-six

/ /

How would I describe a successful life?

/ /

Is there something that is preventing me to become happy?

/ /

What am I going to do today, so that tomorrow is a better day?

/ /

Again, is this life that I am living the life I want to be living?

I AM ENOUGH

Made in the USA
Middletown, DE
10 September 2024

60691430R00116